HOW T CONTROL

OF A

CONTROLLING

RELATIONSHIP

A therapist's perspective

Focus on your feelings. Have faith in these feelings.
Listen to these feelings.

By Kamalyn Kaur

This book is designed to provide helpful information and insight on the subject discussed. Although I am a therapist, I am not your therapist. Reading this book does not create a therapist-client relationship between us. The content of the book is the sole expression and opinion of its author and should not be used as a definitive guide.

The book should not be used as a substitute for the advice of a fully qualified and registered therapist or medical professional. This book is not meant to be used nor should it be used to diagnose, treat or address any medical or psychological condition. For diagnosis or treatment of any medical or psychological issue, please consult with a registered therapist or medical professional.

The author shall not be liable for any physical, psychological, emotional, financial or commercial damages. You are responsible for your own choices, actions and results.

© Kamalyn Kaur, 2019

Index

Preface ...p8

F

- First things First ...p12
- Forcing decisions on you / Pressurising you ...p14
- Family and Friends ...p18
- Fight and Flight ...p22
- Financial Freedom ...p26
- Focus on Feelings ...p32
- Facts ...p36

A

- Awareness ...p46
- Acceptance / Approval ...p50
- Attitude ...p54
- Ambitious ...p60
- Allowed ...p63
- Are you angry or anxious? ...p66
- Actions ...p69

I

- Inner voice ...p74
- Inner strength ...p78
- Intuition ...p81
- It's not me, it's you! ...p86
- I am only doing this because I care/ ...p89
  If I didn't care I wouldn't say it
- I love you ...p92
- Insight ...p96
- I'm a nice person ...p98

T

- Thoughts, feelings and behaviours ...p102
- Thinking ...p104
- Treat you ...p107
- Trying to control you or care for you? ...p110
- Taking care of yourself is not selfish ...p115
- Talking yourself into situations ...p119

H

- Happiness ...p123
- Health ...p127
- Hurt ...p131
- Heal ...p136
- Hate ...p143
- Help ...p146
- Hope ...p150

Closing remarks ...p152

About your Author ...p154

Preface

Faith can be defined as having "complete trust or confidence in someone or something". My question however is why do we need to have this faith in "someone or something?" Why can't we have this faith within ourselves? Why can't we trust or have complete confidence in ourselves?

I am writing this piece of work not as an academic journal and nor is it written as a definitive guide. Instead, it is a piece of writing that has been put together based on my experience of working with clients; life experiences; and observations in both a professional and personal context.

I work as a therapist and come across a diverse range of people who are experiencing a variety of difficulties in their life that stop them from being happy. One of the main reasons that brings people to therapy is difficulties in their relationship or marriage.

Relationships and marriages involve patience; understanding; listening; co-operation; and changing to meet each other in the middle. However, what happens when that change is not a compromise? What happens when that change is something that you don't agree with or don't actually want to do? What happens when that change leaves you feeling that you are no longer the person that you were? What happens when that change leaves you questioning your entire identity? What happens when that change doesn't make you happy?

Those kinds of changes are not a compromise but instead a WARNING SIGN that you are in an unhealthy relationship!

I have worked with individuals who have changed so much in their relationship that they no longer recognise themselves. This change is not something that they have agreed to but instead been forced upon them by their partner or the circumstances created within their relationship. This kind of forced change could be as a result of you being in a controlling / emotionally abusive relationship.

I have also observed patterns, habits and actions that are repeatedly carried out by these individuals, keeping them in toxic situations. More importantly, I understand how an individual can trust their instincts and feelings to be able to overcome and break free of these toxic situations.

To raise awareness and help give you some clarity on your relationship, I have put together some key points, signs, symptoms and examples that can be used as red flags alerting you to the fact that your relationship could be controlling / emotionally abusive.

I have also listed questions that will make you stop, think and reflect on your existing situation. The answers you find might not be what you want to hear and nor will they be easy to accept. However, these answers are not only important but crucial in helping you to create a change. Asking questions and finding answers within yourself will enable you to acknowledge your present situation, and when you are ready, to take the necessary steps that are required for you to be happy.

The book is divided into five main sections.

Each of these sections will cover key areas of a controlling / emotionally abusive relationship, which I believe are important. The five sections and key areas within each of these sections will start with a specific letter.

These five letters will make up the word "faith".

Faith

First Things First

"I don't even know who I am anymore!"

This is one of the most common statements that I hear from a client when they come to see me regarding relationship issues. Compromising within relationships is important and at times necessary, however, not at the detriment of your emotional health and wellbeing. The compromise should be about both of you meeting in the middle, not one person changing every aspect of their life (e.g. likes, dislikes, work, family, friends) from one end of the spectrum to the other. When this happens, you will begin to feel lost and disconnected from yourself.

First things first, let's recalibrate. This will help you be clear about who you are now and who you used to be.

Ask yourself:
- Who was I before this relationship?
- What kind of a person was I?
- What did I like about that person?
- Who am I now?

- How do I feel about this new person?
- What do I like / not like about this new person?
- When did I change from the old me to this new person?
- Why did I change into this new person?
- If I wasn't with my current partner, would I continue being the person that I am?

These questions are difficult to answer and you may not be ready to hear the responses. However, the need to answer these questions is important as it will help you gain a better understanding of your current relationship. They will help you to acknowledge your current situation and move past the avoidance and denial stage that many can often get stuck in.

Forcing Decisions on You / Pressurising You

In a healthy relationship, decisions that have an impact on you both, should be made after discussing it amongst yourselves and considering each other's feelings regarding the decision. A relationship in which decisions are made by your partner without taking into consideration your opinions or feelings can leave you feeling angry; irritable; powerless; insignificant; invaluable; or upset.

These feelings are normal and natural to experience, you are not being irrational or sensitive, although you might find that you are made to feel that you are.

In a controlling / emotionally abusive relationship, your partner will minimise your feelings by making comments such as:

- "It's not a big deal."
- "Why are you making this into such an issue?"
- "Stop making this into a problem."
- "I didn't think you would mind."

- "I didn't realise that you would be so upset."
- "I forgot to ask."
- "I should have checked but I didn't have time."
- "We don't have a choice."
- "Next time I'll make sure to check with you."
- "Why are you getting so angry?"
- "You're overreacting."

These listed comments have the potential to make you believe that what you think or feel isn't important. They also make you doubt yourself and your reaction to the situation. This will result in you backing down, not challenging your partner and eventually complying with the decision that was made by your partner. They get their own way and you will be left finding a way to adjust and adapt to what was decided; sometimes maybe even struggling to do so.

Ask yourself:
- Which comments do I relate to from the list above?
- How often have I heard those comments?
- How are decisions in the relationship made?
- Who makes them and why?

- How do I feel when decisions are made without my involvement?
- Why am I not involved in the decision-making process?
- Given a choice, how would I like the decisions to be made?
- What would my partner say if I asked them to involve me in decisions?
- How do I feel about asking my partner to involve me in future decisions?

This last question is important as it will make you reflect on whether the relationship is based on respect or fear. When asking your partner to change an aspect of their behaviour that is upsetting you, you might feel nervous or on edge about bringing up the topic. Most emotional conversations can be difficult to have or bring up. If however, you are feeling anxious, scared, worried and upset about "causing trouble" or "rocking the boat" or "causing confrontation" or "kicking things off", then you have to ask yourself why you have those concerns.

Is it right that you can't freely express or share how you feel? Is it right that you can't talk about being upset? Is it right that you will ignore what is important to you because you are worried about the consequences of voicing it?

There may be times in a relationship, where one person unknowingly does something that upsets the other. This could be a genuine mistake and after realising how they have upset you, he / she will avoid making the same mistake again. If however, you find yourself in a situation where the same behaviour keeps being carried out despite your partner knowing that it upsets you, then the important question for consideration here is, why do they keep doing it?

In a healthy relationship, respecting the feelings of your other half is normal, natural and to be expected. This includes them not repeating the same behaviours or actions that upset you. This is a given in any healthy relationship, so don't let your partner make you feel that you are being irrational, unfair or asking for too much.

Family and Friends

The start of any relationship is fun, exciting and brings with it promises of new beginnings. During these early stages it is natural to want to spend as much time as possible with this new person in your life. You are investing emotionally into this person as they could be your future.

As time goes on, this person will grow to become a part of your existing family; friends and social circles. This new person should enhance your life and add a new chapter to it, NOT replace existing chapters (unless you want them to).

More often than not, within controlling / emotionally abusive relationships, family and friend circles are no longer present or have drifted away, leaving the individual concerned feeling alone and isolated. These changes can be deliberate and intentional because the less people around you, the easier it is to control you.

Ask yourself:
- How has my relationship with my family changed since this relationship started?

- How has my social life changed since this relationship?
- Why did these changes take place?
- How do I feel about these changes towards my family / social life?
- What do my family and friends say about my relationship / partner?
- What does my partner say about my family and friends?
- How true is what my partner is saying? Where is the evidence to prove this?
- If I had a choice, would I like to have contact / more contact with my family and friends?
- What stops me from being able to do this?

Divide and rule is one of the oldest tactics to control someone. Drip feeding negative or judgemental comments here and there about your family / friends can leave you questioning and doubting the people around you. Some of the common statements to create this rift between you and your existing networks are:

- "They don't like me."
- "I don't like them."
- "You are always spending time with them."

- "You don't care about me."
- "Your family / friends are trying to take you away from me."
- "You have changed."
- "You should spend more time at home."
- "You are being selfish."
- "You only seen them the other day."
- "You're seeing them again?!"
- "They are interfering in our relationship."
- "Do they not have a life of their own?!"
- "Why are they being so possessive?"
- "They aren't good for you."
- "They are trouble. Stay away."
- "But what will I do…."
- "Are you just going to leave me alone….?"
- "Your family / friends are more important than me."
- "So now going out is more important than spending time with me?"

In addition to the these statements, you might also be made to feel guilty or bad about spending time with family and friends by using emotional manipulation e.g. giving you the silent treatment; being moody; passive aggressive behaviour; denying you of certain activities as a form of punishment.

Wanting to spend time with your family / friends is not a privilege or something that you have to earn. You are entitled to do that without any explanation; justification; or permission.

Fight and Flight

The fight and flight response is your natural defence mechanism. It is there to look after you when you are physically in danger or unsafe because fighting off a threat or running away from it could save your life!

The fight and flight response is also triggered off by an emotional threat. When you feel unsafe; insecure; upset; criticised; or judged, your mind tells your body that you are in danger and unsafe. Your natural defence mechanism will be activated and as a result you will start to notice certain changes in your behaviour.

Here are some of the changes within yourself to look out for:
- Frustration.
- Confrontational.
- Short tempered.
- Defensive.
- Irritable.
- On edge / tense.
- Mood swings.
- Avoiding certain places, people or situations.

- Wanting to be alone.
- Not socialising.
- Overthinking / overanalysing.
- Quiet / withdrawn.
- Detached / disengaged / distant.
- Fidgety.
- Unable to concentrate / focus.
- Becoming forgetful.
- Finding it difficult to make decisions.
- Not enjoying activities, socialising, or certain experiences as you did before.

These are just some of the changes that will take place. There are also several physical changes that will take place within your body, covered later in the book. For now, I have listed these ones above as they are the most noticeable ones, making it easier for you to spot. They are also easily noticed by others around you, so even if you were unable to notice them (which is quite common when we are in a state of denial / avoidance / confusion) then at some point or another, someone around you will point it out to you, if they haven't already.

Ask yourself:

- Which of the above behaviours can I relate to?
- How often do I carry out these behaviours?
- Who / what triggers the above behaviours?
- Which environments do I carry out the above behaviours within?
- What am I feeling just before I carry out any of the above behaviours?
- What do I need when I am feeling like that?
- In that moment, what would stop me from carrying out the behaviours?
- When do I NOT carry out these above behaviours?
- Whom do I NOT carry out these behaviours around? Why?

The above questions will help you understand how you are feeling; why you are feeling the way you do; who / what triggers off certain reactions.

Most of the time, a healthy functioning relationship should make you feel happy; emotionally healthy; content; calm; and settled. It is not right nor normal to be constantly feeling irritated, annoyed, angry, unsettled, anxious, upset, distressed or chaotic within a relationship or directly as a result of your partner.

Financial Freedom

Money does not guarantee happiness but at times it can make living life a lot easier. Having money allows you to have the freedom to buy things, socialise, get involved in activities, or experience certain life events that can give you happiness e.g. holidays; travel; live certain lifestyles. In contrast, not having money can also leave you feeling restricted, trapped, stuck, suffocated and limited to what you can or can't do.

This is why one of the easiest and most common way to restrict someone's movement in life or to control where they are going or what they are doing is to cut them off their financial source or restrict access to it.

There are different ways in which this financial freedom can be restricted:

- Constantly questioning you about expenditure and where your money is going.
- Giving you money to spend, almost like giving you pocket money.

- Asking for an account of what has been spent and where.
- Telling you what you can and can't spend money on.
- Checking the prices of items when you have bought them.
- Checking receipts.
- Criticising what you have bought.
- Questioning whether you actually needed to make the purchase.
- Criticising you and judging you for spending money.
- Making you feel guilty for spending money.
- Taking loans or credit cards out under your name.
- Asking you to pay for things and not using their own finances.
- Forcing you to spend money on items that you don't want to spend it on, using your money to purchase it, then the only person that gets enjoyment from it is your partner.

I once worked with an individual whose partner had persuaded her that she needed a new car. To an extent this was true as her existing car had been causing her lots of problems. It was breaking down constantly, regularly being taken to the garage needing repairs or some kind of work done on it. When my client and her partner went to the showrooms to look for cars, my client kept looking for affordable options and ones that wouldn't put extra financial pressure on her as she still wanted to have a quality of life that was "comfortable" and not out of her means. She wanted to continue being able to pay for her gym membership; yoga classes; go out socialising with her friends; and be able to go on holidays – these were the activities and experiences that gave her happiness. Having the finance to be able to pay for it all gave her a sense of freedom and independence.

Her partner convinced her that the cars she was looking at were too old and would cause her the same problems as the current one. There were many conversations had about this but her partner was quite persistent with his argument and even commented on how she doesn't know anything about cars which is why she was "in the mess that you are in now". There were also a few other comments added onto it along the lines of "why are you being so stubborn" and "why are you being difficult".

To avoid confrontation and because she felt completely cornered, my client gave in and purchased the car that her partner suggested. A top of the range sports car which she didn't even feel comfortable driving, as it was too big and powerful for her.

Every day she would take the bus to work despite paying almost £500 every month in repayments, maintenance and fuel for this car. Now we have a situation where not only was she paying for the car but she was also having to pay for her bus fare to and from work.

As time went on, she started cutting back on certain activities e.g. going out for meals; coffee catch ups; holidays; weekend breaks; yoga; and gym membership was cancelled, because she simply couldn't afford that lifestyle anymore. She was cut off and isolated from all the things and people that made her happy.

Until she came to therapy sessions, my client hadn't realised her partner's intention or purpose behind wanting her to purchase this car. The more we explored the relationship issues and the more she spoke about it, the more sense it all began to make until one day in the session my client asked me "Do you think him wanting me to buy that car was his way of keeping my money tied up so that I couldn't continue to be independent?"

That's exactly what it was! Finance was used as a tool to control, isolate and restrict movement.

Ask yourself:

- Who controls the finances in my relationship and why?
- Who takes care of **most** of the expenditure / running of the home? Why?
- What do I pay for / towards in the relationship?
- What does my partner pay for / towards in the relationship?
- How do I feel about that arrangement?
- Am I questioned or critiqued on my finances? How does it make me feel?
- Am I finding myself feeling nervous, anxious or on edge when spending money? If yes then why?
- Am I finding that I am having to hide / lie about purchases?
- Am I finding myself thinking that I didn't even want to spend money on that particular item / make that purchase but felt forced to by my partner?
- How do I feel without financial freedom?
- What have I had to change about my lifestyle due to finance being restricted?

After answering the above questions, you will come to realise how the financial arrangement within your relationship might be impacting on and affecting the quality of your life.

If you are unhappy with the arrangement, then perhaps you can think of what you would like to change about it. If your partner cares and respects you, they will listen to your concerns and feelings around the financial arrangement. If however they are dismissive, disengaged, argumentative, confrontational or don't wish to discuss it at all then these could be signs of an unhealthy relationship.

Furthermore, if you are feeling scared, worried, concerned, nervous, terrified, or sick to your stomach about even bringing up the topic with your partner, then that in itself is very telling about the dynamic of your relationship. In a healthy relationship, communication should take place openly without any feelings associated to fear. It is not right nor normal that you be feeling fearful in a relationship.

Focus on Feelings

Your feelings are your compass in life. There are feelings that are "comfortable" and feelings that are "uncomfortable". The "uncomfortable" feelings are there to tell you that something isn't right or that something needs your attention.

Here is a list of some of the "uncomfortable" feelings that you might experience as a result of being in a controlling / emotionally abusive relationship:

- Irritable.
- Frustrated.
- Angry.
- Anxious.
- Sad.
- Hopelessness.
- Helplessness.
- Emotional / overwhelmed / teary.
- Despair.
- Distress.
- Fear.

- Terror.
- Anguish.
- Gloom.
- Rejection.
- Self-loathing.
- Revulsion.
- Shame.
- Humiliation.
- Resentment.

These feelings are all very powerful and strong feelings, alerting you to the fact that something isn't right. When we have pain in our body, that is our body's way of telling us that something isn't right. We will then address this pain by attending to the source of pain; creating certain changes that can alleviate pain; or seeking medical assistance.

In the same manner, these feelings listed above are all painful feelings causing you discomfort. They need to be acknowledged and the necessary changes will need to be created to address them. If you ignore these feelings, then they begin to manifest as physical symptoms such as:

- Increased heart rate.
- Heart palpitations.
- Tightness in chest.
- Difficulty breathing / breathlessness.
- Stomach cramps.
- Butterflies in stomach.
- Digestive issues e.g. indigestion, irritable bowel syndrome, gastro-intestinal problems.
- Loss of appetite or increase in appetite for certain foods e.g. carbs / sugar.
- Pins and needles in your fingers, hands or toes.
- Numbness or tingling in your fingers, hands or toes.
- Dizzy or light-headed at times.
- Crying / getting upset unexpectantly.
- Fatigue, tiredness or extreme exhaustion.

Ask yourself:
- How many of the above symptoms do I recognise within me?
- (It might be helpful at this point to list them or mark them from the list above)
- When did I first become aware of these symptoms?
- What or who is the reason for these symptoms?

- What triggers these symptoms or makes them worse?
- What makes these symptoms better or lessen?
- How do I deal with these symptoms?
- How effective are my coping strategies at working to reduce these symptoms?
- What impact are these symptoms having on me and my life?
- What would life be like if I didn't have to worry about these symptoms?
- If I could change one thing in my life that I KNOW will reduce these symptoms, what would that change be?

Acknowledging the physical symptoms within your body will not only help you to deal with them but will also make you sit up and think about the reality of your existing situation. It won't be easy, but it is a step in the right direction if you want to begin to feel better.

Facts

"I don't know why I didn't see it sooner."

"How did I not see that?"

"I work in this field; I tell others what to do in these situations."

"I am so good at advising others but why couldn't I see it?!?!"

"I feel so stupid."

"I feel like an idiot."

"The writing was on the wall all along."

"Why did I let this carry on for so long?"

"I should have put a stop to this a lot sooner."

These are some of the statements that I hear from clients. During the therapy sessions, we begin to explore the client's relationship, the different dynamics and aspects of it. The more we unravel and untangle, the more the client comes to realise the gravitas of what has happened or is happening. All of a sudden, it all becomes crystal clear for them and the realisation of the relationship being unhealthy, controlling and abusive begins to set in. The question asked by many is why didn't I see this earlier?

The answer is simple – emotions!

In a relationship, you are thinking emotionally rather than rationally. When you think emotionally, feelings such as guilt, fear, doubt, low self-esteem, low self-confidence and low self-worth come into effect. These feelings make you unsure and uncertain about yourself or the situation that you are in, therefore clouding your judgement and making you overlook what is right in front of you.

The partner carrying out the controlling / emotionally abusive behaviour, may use some the following tactics to confuse you, cloud your judgment or make you doubt yourself:

- Manipulation.
- Lies.
- Denying ever having said / done something.
- Blaming you.
- Turning things around back onto you.
- Playing victim.
- Getting defensive.
- Getting upset when asked a question / challenged.
- Accusing you of bullying them / giving them a hard time.
- Gaslighting.

- Acting hurt, offended or upset about what you have said / done.
- Physically hurting themselves when they are not getting their own way.
- Making you feel guilty for saying no to something or not agreeing with them.
- Highlighting that you are being unreasonable, difficult or stubborn when you say no to something or don't agree with them.

These tactics are introduced gradually and very cleverly into the relationship. You won't even notice how and when it has happened. Before you know it, they become a regular part of the day to day relationship. You may even have found your own way to put up or deal with them.

Self-confidence, self-esteem and self-worth are the pillars upon which we stand, build and grow. Once these pillars have been chipped away at, then we lose the solid foundation upon which we were standing. Once this foundation is broken down, made fragile or been weakened, it is easier to make you believe that you are wrong and that you are to blame for everything going wrong or bad.

You therefore stop questioning or challenging any of the behaviour carried out by your partner, allowing them to continue doing what they are doing to control / emotionally abuse you. This is how the cycle continues, until you are completely exhausted, drained, tired, rundown, unhappy, physically unwell, or SO emotionally distressed that you can no longer continue.

So how do you break this cycle?

You break this cycle by removing emotions from it and thinking rationally. We achieve rational thinking when we start focusing on facts, evidence and proof, rather than relying on memory, past, perceptions or what the controller / abuser is saying.

Facts, evidence and proof don't lie and are harder to misconstrue. Let me give you an example so that this makes a little more sense.

Many years ago, I worked with a client who was terrified of leaving their partner. At first it came across that my client was scared to leave for fear of being hurt, injured or attacked by their partner. As the session continued, I carried on asking different questions to identify what the reason for the underlying fear actually was.

Eventually my client admitted, the fear was of "being left alone, no one caring and not having anywhere to turn to once leaving the marital home". This was the client thinking from a place of fear, insecurity, doubt and uncertainty – all of which had been planted there by the partner. These feelings had kept my client held mentally "hostage" in that relationship for years!

We spoke in great detail about the reality of this statement and how true it actually was, I asked my client to give me *only* evidence and facts to prove that this statement was true. Where was the evidence to prove that no one cares? Where was the evidence to prove that family and friends wouldn't care? Where was the evidence to prove that being homeless was the only option? How did they know that they would have to do everything alone? Where was the proof? When had their family or friends ever abandoned them at a time of need in the past?

All of the replies my client gave were along the lines of:
- "But I just feel...."
- "I think that...."
- "But what if they...."
- "My partner said...."

- "What if…."
- "What would I do if…."
- "I don't know but I just think…."
- "I'm scared in case…."

Those statements are not factual statements, they are all based on assumptions or what you think or feel will happen. None of them are rooted in fact, evidence or proof.

On the contrary, my client was able to give me lots of facts, evidence and examples to prove that on leaving the relationship there **would be** lots of family and friends support around. Furthermore, my client added that if they were being honest, most of the family and friends would be very happy that the relationship had ended because they had never liked the partner. My client also listed all the family and friends who would be more than happy to offer a room until things were resolved and permanent alternative accommodation had been arranged. We also listed all the family, friends, networks, organisations, and professionals that would be available to help my client emotionally during the break-up of this relationship.

Once all the facts had been highlighted, listed and considered, my client's mindset had done a complete 180 turn. Although still feeling raw, vulnerable, upset and fragile, they felt more hopeful and optimistic about being able to deal with life after the relationship.

The approach we used was not a "happy, airy, fairy, let's be positive" approach. Much the opposite - it was realistic, pragmatic and an accurate depiction of what life will be like after the relationship. Not at any stage did we kid ourselves on that it was going to be easy, we both acknowledged and accepted that it was going to be a difficult step. However, the reality was that my client was never going to be doing it alone, the practical support and emotional safety net was going to be there the whole time.

Once this had been realised by the client, their perception of their reality changed. Instead of believing that they would be alone, isolated and abandoned by everyone, they began to realise that they WEREN'T alone; they DID have options; and the reality that had been painted by the partner up until now was in actual fact NOT true or accurate.

It is in this realisation, the "hold" that my client's partner had over them, was released and a sigh of relief was breathed. The shoulders dropped, the tears flowed and my client asks me "Does this mean I can finally be free?"

When you start focusing on facts, evidence and what you see rather than what you think or feel, you will be able to see clearly and accurately. You will see your reality for what it is rather than what has been put into your head by your partner. It is this realisation that will help you release, loosen or let go of this "hold" that your partner has had over you. Mentally you begin to feel that you are no longer stuck, suffocated, trapped or held hostage in that relationship.

Next time your partner says something to you that makes you feel helpless, hopeless, isolated or fearful that you are alone, I want you to ask yourself the questions listed below. Please note, the answers to these questions **need** to be factual and based in evidence so your answers should not begin with "I think…" or "I feel…" as these are emotional statements, not factual.

Ask yourself:

- Where is the evidence to prove what he / she is saying is true?
- Where is the evidence to prove that what he / she is saying is NOT true?
- What would someone else be saying if they were looking in at this situation?
- Would they agree with what my partner is saying?
- Why would they not agree with what my partner is saying?
- What would I say to someone if I was seeing all this happening?
- Why am I not taking on board my own advice?

In asking these questions, you are emotionally taking yourself out of the situation and focusing on facts and evidence. This will help you to think about your situation rationally and logically.

The more rationally and logically you think, the more in control you will begin to feel and the more clarity you will gain over your situation, enabling you to make the decision that is right for you.

F<u>a</u>ith

Awareness

Awareness and self-awareness are both important in order to determine what is going on in your current relationship and the impact it might be having on you. The former is about your external map and the latter is about your internal map. By exercising awareness, you are opening your eyes to your surroundings, environment and the situation you are in. This will enable you to see things clearly, giving you an accurate depiction of your situation. Self-awareness is about opening your third eye and looking inwards at yourself. It is about having an understanding of your thoughts, feelings and behaviours.

More often than not when a relationship is controlling / emotionally abusive it can leave you feeling lost, confused or completely overwhelmed. During times like this, it is easy to be swayed, influenced and questioned to the point where you will begin to doubt yourself. If you can't even trust your own judgement, then how will you know what is right or wrong. How will you know whether certain situations are normal or not? How will you know if certain behaviours are acceptable or not? How will you know if you are right to feel the way that you are or whether you are overreacting? How will you know when you are standing up for yourself or being overly sensitive?

Once you begin feeling like this, it is inevitable that there will be a knock on effect on your self-confidence; self-esteem; and self-worth.

During times like this, your lifeline will be to focus on FACTS! Your opinion, view, perspective, thought or belief can be challenged and misconstrued by others, including your partner. However a fact cannot be challenged, a fact is a descriptive reflection or an account of activities, behaviours or actions that took place. They are based on reality and not on what you *think* or *feel* has happened.

If there is something on your mind that is bothering you but you are unsure about whether you are right to feel the way that you do, then bring your attention and focus onto the facts by asking yourself the following.

Ask yourself:

- Why is this bothering me?
- How do I feel about this?
- Why do I feel this way?
- What would stop me from feeling this way?
- What would this look like from someone else's perspective?
- What would they say about this?
- If someone I loved was describing this situation to me, what would I be saying to them?
- Would I think they were overreacting or being overly sensitive?
- How do I know that this situation is acceptable / not acceptable?
- Why am I doubting how I feel? Where or from whom is this doubt coming from?

These questions will help you step outside of your own mind and look at your situation from a wider perspective. This wider perspective will give you peripheral vision to the situation rather than having a blinkered tunnel vision towards it. This change in perspective will also make you aware of your situation and the feelings going on within yourself as a result of it. You will gain answers that will give you a clear reading of both the external and internal map. Now it is up to you to decide if you wish to roll this map up and put it back in your bag or whether you wish to use this map to help you steer in the right direction.

Acceptance / Approval

In a healthy functioning relationship, your partner will accept you for who you are. They will not change you or accept a version of you that suits them. In a controlling / emotionally abusive relationship your partner will try to change you, mould you, or shape you to appear and behave the way they want you to be. They will also drip feed you with comments to chip away at your confidence, self-esteem and self-worth.

Examples of how this "drip feeding" is done are:
- Criticising you.
- Judging you.
- Constantly picking on you.
- Making remarks about you or what you are doing.
- Making fun of you.
- Making hurtful comments.
- Telling you what you are doing is wrong / unacceptable / bad.
- Using derogatory words.
- Swearing at you.
- Putting you down in front of others.
- Making fun of you in front of others.

Examples of some statements:
- That isn't right....!
- Why do you do that....?
- Have you always done that....?
- Why do you do it that way....?
- That's not how you do it....!
- Do you think that's the right way to do it....?
- I can't believe you do it like that...!
- Why are you such a freak....?
- You're so weird...!
- That's not normal....
- Why are you such a geek...?
- You think you're so smart....!
- Nobody cares what you think...!

It should be noted that criticism isn't always about looks or appearance. It can also be about your abilities, competencies, skills, achievements, successes or intelligence. It might be helpful to note here that the controller / abuser will usually pick on things about you that they feel most threatened or insecure about.

You partner's aim is to leave you feeling as though you are flawed;

imperfect; there is something wrong with you; that you are a bad person; you are not good enough; OR that no matter what you do it will never be good enough.

If you feel worthless and feel that you are not good enough, your confidence will be at an all time low, making it easier for your partner to keep you held hostage in that toxic relationship.

Ask yourself:
- Which of the behaviours listed above does my partner carry out?
- Why does he / she carry out these behaviours?
- What benefits do he / she gain from carrying out these behaviours?
- What does my partner criticise or judge me on? e.g. looks, appearance, skills, job, income?
- How does it make me feel?
- What impact have these behaviours / comments had on my personality and on who I am as a person?
- Who else around me has noticed these changes within me?
- Describe yourself and what kind of person you were before all these behaviours started taking place?

The questions above will help you determine whether your partner accepts you for who you are or whether they accept the version of you that they want you to be. The questions above will also help you to identify and focus on behaviours and comments that over time could have chipped quietly away at your confidence.

Finally, what I will ask you is something which I often ask my clients - if you were so worthless, so bad, so inadequate and so "not good enough" then why did your partner choose to be with you in the first place?

If you are such a disappointment to be around then why are they still with you? What are they getting from sticking around? Who do you know that would put up with the behaviour that you put up with?

The issue here is not that you aren't good enough, the issue here is that you **ARE** good enough. Good enough to make your partner feel insecure; good enough to make them feel threatened; good enough to make them feel intimidated; good enough to make them feel inadequate; and good enough to make them feel that they have to put you down in order to make themselves feel better.

Attitude

Attitude can be defined as a way of thinking or feeling towards something or someone.

When you are in an unhappy relationship, you will notice that your attitude to life and others around you will begin to change. You may begin to feel:

- That the world isn't a safe place.
- It isn't safe to leave the relationship.
- Others are out to get you.
- You are being punished.
- You are a bad person.
- You are not supported.
- You are alone and isolated.
- No one cares.
- You are going to be a nuisance to others.
- You are a burden on others.
- You don't deserve to be happy.
- You are not strong.
- You are worthless.

It is very common to experience these feelings within a controlling / emotionally abusive relationship. Over time, your partner will have chipped away at your confidence, self-esteem and self-worth so much so, that you have no choice but to feel this way. All of the hurtful, criticising and judgemental comments made towards you – although not true – will have begun to feel as though they are true!

This is all part of the strategy of control / abuse. If you feel that you are wrong, bad or at fault then you are less likely to leave the relationship. You could be the strongest person in the world but when we hear something enough times, or when we are told something over and over again, directly or indirectly, then we will eventually begin to believe it. This is NOT a sign of weakness; this is called brainwashing. The only way to stop this from happening is by removing yourself physically away from the source of the brainwashing.

I emphasise this point strongly because a lot of people will continue to put up with and stay within a controlling / emotionally abusive relationship because they are embarrassed or ashamed of letting themselves get into this situation. You didn't let yourself "get into this situation". You have been emotionally manipulated into this situation!

In most cases, the controller / abuser will have put on a façade to entice you into the relationship, make you feel secure, loved, cared for and that you are the best thing ever. As soon as you get comfortable and start to trust this person, then the brainwashing starts in the form of drip feeding you with comments, criticisms, judgements and opinions. All of these tactics will have been used to change your independent, self-reliant, self-assured, and confident attitude to one which is dependent on reassurance, validation or permission from the partner.

Some examples of this dependent behaviour would be:
- Constantly having to check with your partner before making any plans.
- Feeling as though you have to give a detailed breakdown of your day's events.
- Providing details about whom you are meeting, where and when.
- Having to check in throughout the day via texts, phone calls, emails etc.
- Feeling pressure to have your phone on hand for fear of

missing a call / text.
- Asking before purchasing items.
- Justifying your expenditure / spending.
- Seeking approval from partner before wearing certain clothes / makeup.
- Looking at your partner before speaking /expressing an opinion.
- Not taking part in conversations in social settings or when others are around.
- Feeling as though what you have to say isn't important or valuable.
- Feeling worried, stressed or anxious if you are running late / have missed a call / text from your partner.

Now you might look at the behaviours listed above and think that it is not something that will create much of an affect. They might even seem like innocent gestures of love, affection, care and concern expressed on behalf of your partner. However, if you focus on these behaviours and strip them back to what they are actually doing, you will see that each one is taking away your decision making skills; it is taking away your independence; it is making you dependent on someone else's opinion before you take the next step; it is taking away your freedom to move freely in the day; it is taking away your right of choice; it is taking away your ability to decide what you need or want; and the pressure of having to carry out these behaviours will take you away from what you actually want to do. This is when you will begin to feel lost and that you don't know who you are anymore.

Ask yourself:

- What was my attitude like before this relationship?
- What is my attitude like now when in this relationship?
- If there is a change in attitude, when and why is it there?
- What did I believe about the world and others?
- What do I believe now about the world and others?
- What pros does this new attitude have?
- What cons does this new attitude have?
- Do I like the person that I am right now? What do I like about this person?
- Do I like the way I think right now? What do I like about the way I think?
- What would I like to think and be like?
- What / who stops me from thinking and being this way?

These questions will help you reflect on how your attitude might have changed towards yourself; how you see yourself; your relationship; and other aspects of your life.

Ideally, whether you are single or in a relationship, you should like the person that you are. If however you notice that you no longer like yourself since being in your relationship then that can be seen as a red flag that something isn't right within it.

Ambitious

An ambitious individual will have a desire and determination to succeed, whether that is in their personal or professional life. This is a trait that is admirable and can be attractive within an individual. This might even have been one of the traits that your partner initially noticed and liked about you.

However, I would not be surprised if this is one of the traits that has now become an issue or problem. Over years of working with clients within controlling / abusive relationships, what I have noticed and observed is that the very things that your partner liked about you, are the very things that become a potential threat for them.

Any kind of ambition is seen as a potential threat to your controller / abuser. Your ambition is seen as your strength and something that could result in them losing you or not being able to control you.

More often than not, in a controlling / emotionally abusive relationship, I find that individuals who were strong, independent or ambitious are broken down so much that they are left feeling weak, fragile, vulnerable and dependant. They begin to lose confidence in their abilities and competencies resulting in them losing their ambition within certain aspects of life, because these aspects are no longer a priority or of importance

Examples of some of these aspects could be job; career; volunteering; recreational activities; exercising; campaigns; social engagements; etc.

Ask yourself:

- When I met my partner, what was I passionate about in my life?
- What did I want to achieve or pursue?
- Am I still passionate about and in pursuit of these things?
- If so, then what is my partner doing to help / encourage / support me?
- If not, then why am I not passionate about or in pursuit of these things anymore?
- If I had a choice, would I still like to continue following my passions?
- Who or what stops me?
- How do I feel about not being able to pursue my passions in life?

In life, there will be circumstances that require you to change focus or direction e.g. relocation, children, finance, family. That is just life, there will be times that you will have to make adjustments and compromise. However it needs to be just that - an adjustment and compromise - something that you have had time to consider; reflect on; decide on; and be involved in discussing with your partner. If the changes have been forced on you or just expected from you, without giving your opinions or feelings any consideration, then not only is that unfair but it is also a relationship where your opinion is not respected or valued.

A relationship like that will only ever leave you feeling insignificant; worthless; and invaluable. That is not a healthy relationship.

Allowed

The key to a happy and healthy relationship is communication. Checking with your partner before making a plan. Running things past your partner before making a decision. Taking into consideration how your partner feels about a certain situation or event before you get involved in it. These all are what we can describe as being normal things to do when we are in a relationship. It is a sign of respect and consideration towards the other person.

In this section, I am not referring to the aforementioned examples. I am referring to the times where you feel you need "permission" to do things; see people; go places. I am referring to situations where if your partner said "NO" then you would feel you had no choice other than to oblige. In some cases, you may even find yourself thinking or saying that:

- "For the sake of keeping peace I'll just go with their decision."
- "I can't be bothered arguing so I'll just agree or not say anything."
- "It wasn't that important so I can just leave it."
- "I didn't even want to do that thing / go to that place."

- "It's really not a big deal."
- "It doesn't matter it's not important."
- "I don't want to be confrontational or argumentative."
- "This will just end up in an argument so what's the point?"
- "I don't want to rock the boat."
- "I don't want to cause trouble."
- "It's not worth the hassle."

If you have ever found yourself saying any of the above statements, then it might be a red flag to the fact that you are possibly in a controlling / abusive relationship where your partner "decides" what you do; when; and with whom.

Think about the last time you wanted to do something, be involved in an activity or wanted to go somewhere to which your partner said no and answer the following questions.

Ask yourself:
- If it wasn't for my partner saying no would I have done what I wanted to / carried out the activity / gone where I wanted?
- How did I feel when my partner said no?
- What was their reason for saying no?

- What do I think my partner gained by saying no?
- What would have happened if I ignored their decision?
- How do I feel about ignoring their decision and doing what I want to do?
- How often does my partner seek my permission?
- When was the last time I stopped my partner from doing something?
- What happens when I stop my partner from doing something they want to do?
- What would my life be like if I didn't have to seek permission from my partner?

The questions above will make you focus on the dynamics of your relationship. It will also help you identify if your relationship is fair or whether there is a power imbalance within it. Remember power is about control, if your partner has more power in your relationship that means they have more control within the relationship. Something which you now have to decide whether you are happy about or not.

Are you angry or anxious?

Anger and anxiety are two sides of the same coin. The anger is your "fight" response whilst anxiety is your "flight" response! When you feel hurt; upset; insecure; vulnerable; distressed; judged; criticised; intimidated; or nervous – you will react in one of these two ways. The response that you do will be determined by your personality, the circumstances and how threatened you are feeling in that moment.

If naturally you are a person that avoids confrontation or arguments then there is a high chance that your default position will not be the "fight" response. You are most likely to withdraw, go quiet, take a step back or retreat – all behaviours commonly related to anxiety, which is your flight response. If you are a person who isn't adverse to arguments then you are more likely to revert to the "fight" response in controlling / emotionally abusive situations. Your behaviour therefore will be more based on anger e.g. aggressive body language, raised voices, argumentative, confrontational, defensive, or retaliation.

It is important to note here that within a controlling / emotionally abusive relationship what can often happen is that you could have initially had the "fight" response leaving you feeling angry. However, as time has gone on, you might have noticed that the "fight" has left you. Instead you now find yourself reverting to the "flight" response and nestling feelings of anxiety rather than anger.

In any case, both sets of feelings are not healthy nor normal to have within a relationship or directly as a result of your partner. If you are in a happy, healthy and secure relationship then why should any of those feelings be arising for any length of time.

Ask yourself:
- How often do I feel angry / anxious?
- When do I feel this emotion?
- Why do I feel it?
- What are the triggers?
- Is this a new emotion that I am experiencing, or has it always been there?
- When did I first become aware of this emotion?
- How does this emotion impact on my physical health?
- When is this emotion not there?
- What other areas of my life do I notice this same emotion? e.g. family, friends, work?

- If I do notice it in other areas of my life, then why is it there?
- If I notice that it is NOT present in other areas of my life, then why is it NOT there?

Anger and anxiety are strong emotions. Both these emotions are a warning bell or red flag that something isn't right. They are alerting you to the fact that you are unsafe, feeling insecure or unsettled, so you have to get out or you have to change your situation until you do feel safe and secure.

Actions

"Actions speak louder than words."

This is a saying that is very dear to me and I strongly believe that there is not another statement truer than this.

An emotionally abusive / controlling relationship can be very overwhelming, confusing and contradicting - leaving you feeling lost, unsure, doubtful and questioning your judgement. At times when you are feeling like this, the best thing to do is to stop concentrating solely on the words being said but instead focus on the actions of the other person too.

KEY QUESTION: IS WHAT THE PERSON SAYING ALIGNED WITH THEIR ACTIONS?

If your partner tells you that they love you; care for you; and they would do anything for you - are their actions aligned with what they say?
- What do they do to show you they love or care for you?
- Do you feel loved / cared for when they carry out these actions?

- When do they carry out these actions?
- Is it a regular ongoing behaviour within your relationship? Or is it typically after an argument or out of guilt?

Your partner tells you that you are important.
- Do you feel important in their life?
- How often do you feel important in their life?
- What do they do to make you feel important?
- How can you prove using facts and evidence that you are important to your partner?

Your partner tells you that it is important for you to be happy.
- How often do you feel happy in that relationship?
- Why do you feel happy?
- What does your partner do to make you feel happy?
- What do they do when you are unhappy?
- How often do you feel unhappy within your relationship?
- What are the reasons for you being unhappy within your relationship?

Your partner tells you that they respect and value you.
- What do they do within the relationship to make you feel respected and valued?
- How are decisions made in the relationship? Does a discussion take place or is a decision just delivered to you?
- Are you asked to do things or just told to do them?
- How often are your feelings taken into consideration?
- What happens if you say no to something? Are you heard?
- What happens when you voice your opinion or view on a matter? Does it get taken on board?

Your partner is telling you that you're not good enough, constantly criticising you and making you feel that you are flawed or at fault. If that is the case, then:
- Why is your partner still with you?
- Why doesn't your partner leave?
- What does your partner gain from staying in that relationship?

Your partner tells you that no one will have you; take you; like you; put up with you; accept you; be able to live with you then WHY ARE THEY? Let's look at this realistically, if you were SO unbearable then why are they sticking around? Let's focus on what is actually going on in this relationship!

- What are they getting out of staying with you? e.g. financial security, emotional security, place to stay
- What would happen if your partner wasn't getting those benefits in the relationship anymore?
- Has there ever been a time when you decided to walk away or asked your partner to walk away from the relationship?
- If so, how did your partner react? What did they do or say?
- How would your partner function / or carry on in life without you? Do they have the means (e.g. finance, house, car, job etc) to function?
- What was your partner's life like before they met you?

This section is important as it encourages you to focus not just on what is being said by your partner but also to focus on what is being done by them and the reasons why. When we start focusing on actions and not just words then it creates a new dimension to the relationship. It allows you to take a step back and look at your relationship from a wider perspective which means you will be able to see into the blind spots to notice things that you may have missed or overlooked.

Faith

Inner voice

Your inner voice is your compass in life - guiding you; directing you; telling you right from wrong; speaking what your heart desires; and keeping you on track. That inner voice is there to look out for you and is making sure that you are safe, secure and happy. That voice is usually what is screaming out at you when something isn't right or good for you.

This inner voice tells you:
- Something is off kilter.
- This isn't right.
- This is not normal.
- You don't deserve this.
- I can't believe this is happening.
- I feel trapped.
- I feel stuck.
- I want to get out.
- This is a nightmare.
- What have I got myself into?
- This is happening too fast.
- Is this right?

- I feel like I am not in control.
- What is happening?
- I'm not happy.
- I'm scared.
- Get out.
- Something doesn't add up.
- It is not making sense.

These are some of the common statements that I have heard my clients say during their therapy sessions. In their first session they will say, I should have known, there was a little voice in my head, but I just ignored it. That little voice is usually one of the above statements. More often than not, that little voice is ignored or pushed aside, but why?

It can be scary acknowledging, accepting and admitting that you are unhappy. As soon as you acknowledge it or say it out loud then it is no longer in your head, it becomes real. When something becomes real then it makes it harder to ignore. So if we aren't ready to accept or acknowledge something in our life then it is easier to suppress the inner voice by telling ourselves that:

- I'm being overly sensitive.
- I'm overanalysing.
- I'm reading too much into it.
- I'm making a big deal out of nothing.
- It's too late to say anything.
- What will other people say?
- I'm being silly.
- It's not as bad as what it seems.
- It might get better.
- It is not always like this.
- I will just wait to see if things improve / get better.

That inner voice is important. Your inner voice tells you when your emotional needs of love, care, attention, connection and compassion have not been met. By ignoring it, you are ignoring your emotional needs. That inner voice is your red flag telling you that something OR someone isn't right in your life. It is alerting you to the fact that there is a part of your life that requires your attention and action.

However, what most people will do is to ignore it and drown out this little voice by making ourselves busy in the hustle bustle of life; avoiding the issue that requires fixing; distracting ourselves from what is going on inside our head; or making the issue insignificant.

<u>Ask yourself:</u>

- How do I currently feel about my situation?
- Why do I feel this way?
- What / who makes me feel this way?
- How do I want to feel?
- What would life be like if I wasn't in this situation?
- If someone I loved told me they felt this way, what would I be saying to them?

Start paying attention to this inner voice. It will be scary and difficult to do so but it is very important if you want to be emotionally happy, healthy and stress-free.

Inner Strength

There are a number of reasons why individuals will continue to stay in a relationship despite knowing that it might not be right for them. Some of the reasons are that they love the person; worry they won't be able to go on; think they can't survive; believe they won't cope without the relationship; feel guilty about leaving the partner; or have guilty feelings around the impact it may have on others, particularly any children in that situation. In extreme cases, there may also be a FEAR of the partner, so the worries will be around being hurt; what the other person will do; how the other person will react; what they might take away; or how they might make life difficult in the future.

It is understandable how the above listed reasons will keep you in a situation. However what you are currently doing is underestimating your own ability and competency to be able to deal with difficult situations. In relationships which are controlling / emotionally abusive, it is common for the individual experiencing the controlling / abusive behaviour to lose focus of what they are capable of and able to achieve. During times like this you have to remind yourself of your own inner strength and resilience.

Ask yourself:

- What other difficult situations have I experienced in my life?
- How did I deal with those situations?
- What did I do well in those situations?
- What did I do to help me deal with those situations?
- What skills / qualities helped me deal with those situations?
- How could those skills / qualities help me deal with my present situation?
- Who else could I ask for help?
- What other support do I need to help me deal with the present situation?

Asking yourself these questions will aid in building your self-confidence as you will be focusing on what you CAN do rather than focusing on what you CAN'T do. More often than not, in controlling / emotionally abusive relationships, you will have been continuously criticised and repeatedly told or made to feel that you aren't good at this; rubbish at that; can't achieve things in life; you're good for nothing; or that you are not good enough.

You will, without even consciously being aware, have taken on the voice of your partner. So even when he / she aren't there, you will continue that toxic chat within you own head. This is the chat that will disempower you, keep you stuck and stop you from moving forward or away from that relationship. Exactly what your partner will want!

By focussing on the answers of the questions above, you are enabling yourself to remove the blinkers and look at things from a wider perspective. A perspective that is more accurate and reflective of what is actually going on rather than living with the thoughts that have been put into your mind. This change in perspective is what will then create a catalyst for change within your mindset and consequently your situation too.

Intuition

- "Something doesn't feel right."
- "I can't put my finger on it."
- "I feel uneasy."
- "I'm not sure."
- "I don't know why but this doesn't feel right."
- "I feel it's going to be a mistake."
- "This is not right."
- "Something is holding me back."
- "I feel unsettled."
- "Something isn't sitting right with me."
- "I am not comfortable with this."
- "I feel on edge."

Most of the time we make decisions based on analysis; research; information; practicality; logic; and the right thing to do. However, what happens when logically and rationally it is the right thing to do but it just doesn't "feel right". That feeling is your intuition, commonly known as your gut feeling. It is the feeling that comes from within and makes you feel unsettled, unsure, uncertain, wary and unsafe. That feeling is telling you that something isn't right and not to go ahead or continue with that particular situation. If ignored, this feeling will manifest itself physically in your body. The two most common areas of your body to be affected and also the most noticeable when affected are your chest and stomach. Some of the physical symptoms you will notice will be:

Stomach:
- Indigestion.
- Reflux.
- Churning in tummy.
- Butterflies.
- Cramps.
- Feeling bloated.
- Loss of appetite.
- Increase of appetite.
- Digestive problems.
- Irritable Bowel Syndrome.
- Diarrhoea.
- Constipation.
- Feeling sick / nauseous.

Chest:
- Heart racing.
- Heart palpitations.
- Breathlessness.
- Difficulty in breathing.
- Shallow breathing.
- Holding breath without realising.
- Tightness in chest.
- Pain in the chest area.
- Feeling suffocated.
- Panic attacks.

Let's get practical – do the following:

When you are feeling chaotic and have a million thoughts running through your mind, it is not easy to focus; center yourself; be mindful or practise meditation. However, these are the very times that it *is* important for you to anchor yourself and focus on what is going on inside you. I understand that it might be difficult, but it is not impossible.

Here are a few tips that will help you to ground yourself:

- Choose a time and place where you won't be disturbed or distracted.
- I know life is busy, but you will have to MAKE time for this to enable you to focus on your present situation.
- You might have reasons why this is not achievable or possible for you. Are they really reasons or are they excuses because you aren't ready to deal with your present situation?
- Close your eyes. Take a deep breath in through your nose. Keep going until you feel that your lungs are filled, and you can no longer continue to breathe in.
- Now breathe out through your mouth. Breathe out slowly, controlled and as though you are blowing out candles on a cake. I want you to push all that air out until you feel that your lungs are empty.
- Now do this again. Repeat 6 times.
- At this point you will be feeling calmer and relaxed. If not, then repeat the breathing 6 times again.
- Now think about your life and being honest with yourself, identify the part of your life that is making you feel unsettled.
- Why do you think the unsettled feeling is there?

- If this unsettled feeling could talk, what would it be telling you?
- How does it make you feel?
- Where do you feel this in your body?
- When did you first notice this unsettled feeling?
- How do you deal with this unsettled feeling?
- What would make this feeling go away?
- What would life be like if this unsettled feeling wasn't there?

All of the above questions will help you to focus in on your intuition and listen to it. Up until now, either knowingly or unknowingly, you may have ignored this intuition. This is completely understandable as it is not easy to accept or acknowledge an upset feeling.

However, what I know about intuition is that that feeling will never disappear. It will always be there, niggling away in the back of your mind or sitting in the pit of your stomach. Left unattended, it will manifest physically as a discomfort or illness in your body. The only way it will leave is if you deal with the reason for it being there in the first place. By ignoring it, all you are doing is putting off the inevitable.

It's not me, it's you!

In a controlling / emotionally abusive relationship the behaviour of deflection takes place all the time.

Deflection is a tactic used by the controller / abuser to place the focus, blame and legitimacy of actions on you. In doing so, they will misdirect attention away from themselves and what they have done. They will be unable to focus on their behaviour and instead will aim a barrage of argument and blame on you, taking away from the original point that you might have made or wanted to discuss.

Some of the common statements used when deflecting are:
- What about the times when you do......!
- If it wasn't for you, I wouldn't behave this way!
- You make me do this!
- You make me feel this way!
- It's your fault that this happened!
- It's always my fault!
- You always blame me!
- You feel upset...what about me, how do you think I feel?
- You are so selfish.

- You have changed.
- You are not the same person anymore.

Often what happens is that the controller / abuser will not even listen to what you say, nor will they be able to focus on what is being discussed at that point in time. They will blame their behaviour and actions on you, playing the victim themselves as if they are the one who has been hard done by. Often, situations / events from the past will be brought up and used as argument points. The essence of what should actually be discussed or the point that you wanted to raise will then be lost amongst this verbal attack.

Ask yourself:
- Do I feel heard?
- Do I feel understood?
- Does my partner listen to what I have to say?
- Do I feel like my feelings matter in this relationship?
- Is my opinion taken on board or considered?
- Do I sometimes stop myself from saying anything because I know it will be ignored?
- Does my partner talk over me when I am in the middle of expressing my feelings?

- Am I constantly apologising for things that are not my fault?
- Do I find myself making excuses for my partner's behaviour?
- Is my partner always the victim, no matter what the situation?
- Do I feel that, in this relationship, my emotions matter as much as my partner's?
- If the answer is no, then why are my partner's feelings more important that mines?

In this section, I am asking you to reflect on the enlisted statements and identify how many of them are familiar to you and regularly used within your relationship by your partner. Furthermore, the questions listed have been designed to help you clarify your position within your relationship as they will help you to identify whether your feelings are important, heard or even acknowledged within your relationship. If not, then it could be said that there is a power imbalance within the relationship.

How you feel is important, it matters, and it is relevant. Asking for your feelings to be considered by your partner is not an unrealistic or high expectation – that is normal, natural and to be expected within a healthy relationship.

I am only doing this because I care / If I didn't care I wouldn't say it

Another classic line or statement commonly used by the controller / abuser within a relationship is, "I am only doing this because I care" OR "If I didn't care I wouldn't say it." (If I could insert a rolling eye emoji here, I would.)

This statement might be true. However, if you really care about someone, you say and do things without hurting their feelings and disrespecting them. You don't put them down, criticise them, mock them, judge them, pressurise them, get jealous by them, chip away at their confidence, bring their self-esteem down OR make them question their self-worth.

That is not caring behaviour. That is CONTROLLING behaviour!

Ask yourself:

- Do I feel "cared for" in this relationship?
- Who else in my life cares about me?
- Make a list of these people.
- How do I know they care about me?
- How do they speak to me?
- What do they say to me?
- What tone do they use when they speak to me?
- Do they talk and treat me in the same manner as my partner?
- What would these people who care for me say if they witnessed what was being said or done by my partner?
- How do I feel about the comments / behaviours of my partner?
- Does it feel the comments / behaviours are coming from a place of care or criticism and cruelty?
- Is that how I would speak or behave towards someone that I cared for?
- If no, then why not?
- If you think that it is not acceptable to treat others like that, then why is it ok for you to be spoken to or treated like that?

Do the following:

- Take out a minute. Close your eyes.
- Think about someone that you are really close to and feel very protective towards.
- Think about some of the comments, statements, words that were / have been used towards you by your partner.
- Now think about the behaviours that were / have been used against you by your partner.
- Keeping your eyes closed, imagine these words and behaviours being used against the person that you feel really close to and protective over.

Now consider this:

- How does it make you feel?
- What would you say to them?
- What would you advise them to do?
- Why does the same advice not apply to you?
- What makes you different to the person that you are advising?

I love you

In a healthy relationship, you will feel loved in a way that enables you to live your life freely. If you are feeling stuck, trapped or suffocated in this relationship then this could be an indication that you are in a controlling / emotionally abusive relationship.

A healthy relationship is one that enhances your existing life - it adds value, substance, meaning and happiness to what is already existing. If you find yourself having to remove or get rid of other areas of your life e.g. family, friends, socialising, fitness, work - to make room for the relationship then you need to stop and reflect on this situation.

Ask yourself:
- What was my life like before this relationship?
- How did I feel about my life?
- What did I enjoy the most?
- How has life changed since my partner has come into my life?
- Why did those changes take place?
- Who is responsible for these changes?
- How do I feel about those changes?

- Do I still engage in the activities that I enjoyed the most before this relationship?
- If not, then why not?
- What is stopping me from reconnecting with these areas of my life that I have lost since being in this relationship?
- If it wasn't for these things / persons / circumstances stopping me, would I like to reconnect with these areas of my life again?

In my line of work, I have seen a lot of emotional blackmail and emotional manipulation take place within relationships under the label of "love". Here is what it sounds like:

- "Are you going to see your friends again?"
- "You only seen your family / friends the other day?"
- "I don't like your family / friends."
- "I think they are using you."
- 'Why do you even bother with them?"
- "You don't have any time for me."
- "You don't love me."
- "I want you all to myself."
- "We don't spend any time together."

- "Do you not want to spend time with me?"
- "I'm not important."
- "Everyone else is more important."
- "You've changed."
- "You're not the same person anymore."
- "You don't care about me."

It can be confusing to make sense of these statements because at times you will start to question whether there is any truth in them. You will begin to doubt yourself, overthink, overanalyse, feel guilty and consequently second guess whether you are doing the right thing.

During times like this, take out a few minutes to reflect on the situation. Think about the situation in a rational, logical and calm manner instead of thinking about it from a point of emotion.

- Focus on facts and evidence, is there any truth to what your partner is saying?
- Where is the evidence to prove that this is true?
- Where is the evidence to prove that this is not true?
- Is your partner's behaviour coming from a place of love, care and concern?

- Or is their behaviour coming from a place of insecurity, jealously, unkindness, cruelty?

It is important to note that in an unhealthy, controlling / emotionally abusive relationship, the person's behaviour will be clingy, inflexible, impatient, unkind, jealous, insecure, craving attention, attention seeking, selfish, greedy, egotistic. These feeling can result in an individual making a lot of comments, statements and accusations that are untrue or not founded in any reality. All of the questions above will help with you being able to rationalise and put things into context.

Insight

Insight is important to help you to understand a person. At the start of any relationship, most people will put their best foot forward - it is all about impressing you, letting you see how nice they are, what a good person they are. If this behaviour is genuine then it will continue and carry on past the honeymoon stages of dating / early stages of the relationship. If however things start to change then this is something that you could explore further to gain a better understanding of what the person is really like.

Some things you may want to consider, explore or gain a better understanding about are:

- What was my partner's past relationships like?
- How has my partner described their past relationships?
- What was the reason for those relationships coming to end?
- How does my partner speak about ex partners? What does that tell me?
- What is my partner's relationship like with their family / friends?
- Is there any patterns or similarities between the past

relationships?
- If so, what are they?
- Are any of those patterns or similarities present in my relationship?

The answers to these above listed questions will give you a better understanding of the character; personality; and traits of your partner. It's almost like you will be gathering pieces of a puzzle and once you have put all the pieces together you will be able to see the full picture. Not just the parts your partner wants you to see.

I'm a nice person

This statement rings alarm bells for me. This is one of the first things that my client will say when they start coming to therapy regarding a controlling / emotionally abusive relationship. I thought they were a nice person. They seemed like a nice person. They told me how they were a nice person.

If someone keeps telling you they are a "nice person" - it could be an innocent fleeting statement or if delved into a little deeper, could be something to reflect on and explore a bit more in detail. If someone is a nice person then this will be evidenced and showcased in all that they do; their actions; and their behaviours. They shouldn't have to keep saying this. If someone keeps saying this repetitively then it's worth considering whether they are saying this to convince you OR in some cases almost even to convince themselves that they are.

In situations like this - actions speak louder than words. Stop believing and engaging with the words but instead start focusing on facts and evidence by drawing your attention to their actions instead.

Ask yourself:

- What has my partner done that suggests to me that they are a nice person?
- What are they like and how do they behave within their circle of family / friends?
- How does my partner speak to others?
- How do others respond to my partner?
- What is my partner like and how do they speak to me when things don't go their way?
- Is my partner a nice person all the time or only when it suits them or when things are going their way?
- What facts and evidence do I have to prove that they are a nice person?
- What facts and evidence do I have to prove that they are NOT a nice person?
- Do I believe my partner when they say that they are a nice person?
- Do I really believe it OR do I just want to believe it but deep down inside I actually have an unsettling feeling?

The questions above are structured in a way where you are forced to focus on the actions and the reality in front of you rather than believing and engaging with what has been drip fed over the weeks, months or years within that relationship to you by your partner.

Faith

Thoughts, feelings and behaviours

When you are in a controlling / emotionally abusive relationship, as time goes on, your thoughts will begin to change. The reason for this is because you will begin to feel stuck, trapped, suffocated, and experience a sense of hopelessness or helplessness as you can't find a way out of your situation.

Your thoughts may become any of the following:
- Negative.
- Always focusing on what has gone wrong rather than what has gone right.
- Making predictions about the future.
- Self-critical.
- Judgmental towards yourself.
- Extremely black and white, with no room for any grey areas.
- Confused.
- Always expecting the worse.
- Waiting for something bad to happen.
- Limiting and controlled, therefore not getting too excited

about anything in case you "jinx" something.
- Irrational.
- Making mountains out of molehills.
- Destructive.
- Unhelpful.

<u>Ask yourself:</u>
- Which ones do I relate to? (make a list of them)
- How long have I had these types of thoughts?
- What were my thoughts like before? e.g. calmer, happier, clearer, rational, relaxed, positive?
- Why did they change?
- How do I feel about this change?
- What would help me to change back to the way I was or used to think?

It is very important to become aware of your thoughts and what sort of thoughts you have. Our thoughts create feelings. Pay attention to these feelings. It is these feelings that are your compass in life; steering you in the right direction; telling you when you have come off track; and telling you when something isn't right or needs your attention.

Thinking

There is a difference between a "thought" and "thinking". For the purposes of this section, I will distinguish between the both.

A thought is an idea or opinion which occurs within our mind. Thinking is the process that is involved in order to create the actual thought.

When we are happy, safe, secure, content and settled, then our thinking is calm, controlled, clear, rational, logical, and mindful. However, when we are unhappy, unsafe, insecure, discontent, unsettled or in a stressful relationship, our thinking will be chaotic, overwhelming, confusing, irrational, emotional, and projecting into the future.

Here are some of the unhelpful thinking habits that you might develop:
- Overthinking.
- Overanalysing.
- Overreacting.
- Overwhelming.
- Repetitive thoughts.

- Repeating or replaying certain conversations / scenarios in your mind.
- Certain thoughts are on loop in your mind.
- Focusing on the past.
- Projecting into the future.
- Imagining what it would be like in the future.
- Making predictions about certain scenarios / situations.
- Creating scenarios in your mind that have not yet happened.

<u>Ask yourself:</u>

- Which unhelpful thinking habits from list above do I relate to? (make a list of them)
- How long have I been thinking this way?
- What makes me think this way?
- How does this way of thinking affect my health?
- How does this way of thinking impact on my life? What areas does it impact on? e.g. work, social life, family time?
- What would my life be like if I didn't think this way / in these ways?
- What was my thinking like before it changed?
- What would help me to change back to the way I was?

It is easier to blame our thinking habits on life events, work life, day to day stresses of life or running a family home. Asking yourself the above questions will help you crystallise the actual source of your unhelpful thinking habits and perhaps help you to see that the source might actually be a lot closer to home - your relationship.

In doing so, you will be taking a step closer to accepting that perhaps your present relationship situation needs attention. No more denial or avoidance. No one finds it easy to step out of their comfort zone however you won't change, move, progress or grow unless you do.

Treat you

This section is about "HOW" your partner treats you. So you met your partner, they were charming, funny, thoughtful, considerate, helpful. Some time goes by and none of these traits are present anymore within the relationship. When someone is genuine and being real, the way they treat you will stay the same and preferably get better as time goes on. If how they treat you begins to deteriorate or get worse as your relationship begins to progress, then you have to ask yourself the question - which version of this person is real? Is it the one that you met initially or is it this one now?

To make an impression, people put their best foot forward. As time goes on and the person begins to feel more comfortable around you, their true likes, dislikes and preferences will begin to reveal. You'll see versions of them that weren't initially there - maybe they aren't as tidy as you thought; they don't want to go out for meals as much anymore; they prefer to stay indoors rather than go out socialising; or maybe they can't cook as well as you thought. There are some things you can overlook and what you can overlook is going to be unique to every individual. That is your decision to make.

However not at any point should the change in this person entail you being disrespected or mistreated.

Ask yourself:
- What was my partner like when we first met?
- What is my partner like now?
- What has changed from when I first met them?
- What is different now about the way they treat me?
- Is the treatment different when others are around?
- What are the behaviours towards me like when others are around?
- What is different about the behaviour when others are around as opposed to when we are alone?
- What would my partner say or do if I treated them the way they treat me?
- How would I feel if a friend / family member / daughter / son was treated this way?
- Would I allow them to continue being treated this way?
- If no, then why do I allow myself to be treated in this way?

It is not easy to admit that there might be something wrong in your relationship, however it is very important for you to acknowledge what is going on. It is only then that you can take any necessary steps or actions that might be required to create a change.

Trying to control you or care for you?

Are you being controlled without even knowing that you are?

When we think of being controlled, automatically we think that it would include obvious behaviours such as violence or aggression. However, at times this control can be so discreet, disguised and hidden within feelings of love, care and affection that it can go unnoticed.

These are some of the ways in which you could be controlled by your partner. He / she:

- Tells you what to buy and in some cases where to buy it too.

- Tells you what you should say and how you should say it.

- Criticises you and judges you.

- Comments on your appearance negatively.
  - You look better when you wear….
  - I don't like your hair like that….
  - I don't like it when you wear clothes like that.
  - You look better in this.
  - Don't you have anything else?
  - Are you going out looking like that?
  - You look silly.
  - That looks weird.
  - You are so embarrassing.
  - I don't want to be seen with you.

- Comments on your clothes.
  - I don't like this on you.
  - I don't like the way it fits.
  - It doesn't suit you.
  - I don't like that style.
  - Why are you wearing that?
  - That's not even in fashion.
  - Do you have to wear that?
  - Why don't you try this instead?

- Tells you how to behave when you are outside.
  - Don't talk too much.
  - Make an effort.
  - Don't just sit there quietly.
  - Don't talk to them because they don't like you.
  - Don't talk to them because you will bore them.
  - Don't talk about your job they aren't interested.
  - Don't tell them what you do for work, it's so embarrassing.
  - Don't ask too many questions.
  - Stay next to me and don't walk away.

- Minimises your feelings.
  - Ignoring you when you are talking.
  - Continuing to carry out a behaviour that they know annoys or upsets you.
  - Walking away from you when you are upset.
  - Not comforting you when you are upset.
  - Making fun of you when you are upset / emotional.
  - Telling you that you are blowing things out of context or making a big deal out of nothing.
  - Laughing when you are upset / emotional.
  - Telling you that how you feel isn't important.

- Talking about their own feelings when you are in the middle of discussing yours.
- Not listening to your opinion.
- Asking you for your opinion and then doing the complete opposite.
- Asking you for your advice or opinion and then telling you that it is stupid or silly.

There are a lot of behaviours listed above that can be carried out as a means of controlling someone. However, there are a lot of the behaviours listed above that can also be because your partner has your best interests at heart and genuinely cares for you.

It can be difficult to identify whether the behaviour is there because they are trying to control you or because they care. To help you out and determine which one it is, I have put together a few questions.

Ask yourself:

- How does my partner's behaviour make me feel?
- Does it make me feel loved, cared for, respected?
- Or does it make me feel annoyed, irritated, upset, meaningless, criticised, disrespected, worthless?
- What would happen if I went against my partner's behaviour and instead done what I wanted to?
- Would my partner get annoyed, angry, upset, ignore, or give me the silent treatment if I went against what they wanted me to do?
- If yes, then why would they do that if they really loved me and wanted what is best for me?

It is important to remember that when someone loves and cares for you, they ultimately want you to be happy. If they are only happy when things go according to their plans or the way they want to do them, then that behaviour is embedded within control not care.

<u>Taking care of yourself is not selfish</u>

Taking care of yourself is not selfish. Having some "me time" is not only nice to have but is also essential for your emotional health and wellbeing. Taking time out for yourself allows you to recharge your batteries; re-energise; and restore your energy levels.

In a controlling / emotionally abusive relationship this "me time" will be even more important as it will allow you to take a step back from your situation and look at it from a different perspective. This is the very thing that the controller / abuser will be afraid of, so they will try their best to ensure that you don't get any "me time". Some of the ways they will make sure they do this is by:

- Not leaving you alone.
- Constantly calling you when you are out.
- Checking up on you when you are out.
- Making an excuse or finding a reason for you to come home if you are out.
- Asking you lots of questions when you have to go out.
- Questioning your plans.

- Wanting to know who you are going out with.
- Constantly asking you to do things when they see you sitting down or taking a break.
- Watching you struggle to do things but not helping.
- Criticising you for taking time out for yourself.
- Telling you that you are selfish for asking for some time to yourself.
- Laughing at you when you say you want some "me time".
- Belittling your need for "me time".
- Making condescending comments regarding "me time".
- Deliberating interrupting you when you have asked to be left alone.
- Not offering to help even though you might look like you are busy or rushed off your feet.

Ask yourself:
- When was the last time I had "me time"?
- How did I feel after it?
- What were the benefits for me?
- What impact does "me time" have on my emotional health?
- What was my partner's behaviour towards me the last time I had "me time"?

If you feel that you don't need "me time", ask yourself:

- Why do I not feel the need to have "me time"?
- Have I always felt like this towards "me time"?
- What / who stops me from having "me time"?
- What thoughts stop me from having "me time"?
- Do those thoughts belong to me or am I just echoing what my partner has said?
- What would I like to do if I DID have "me time"?

Taking time out for yourself is important and for many it is a welcomed break. However if you are scared of what is going on inside your head and don't want to think about certain situations, then convincing yourself that "me time" isn't important could be a form of avoidance in dealing with your current situation.

Sometimes, your partner has broken you down so much that you subconsciously begin to feel and believe that you don't deserve time to yourself or that you are not worthy of nice experiences.

This section is structured to help you identify all the ways in which your partner could be prohibiting you from any "me time"; the impact that this is all having on you; and uncover the underlying reasons as to why you are not opting to give yourself time out.

Talking yourself into situations

In a healthy relationship, you will participate and get involved in activities; experiences; and life events because you ***want to*** and not because you feel that you **SHOULD / HAVE TO.**

When you do things because you feel that you should / have to, it means that you are feeling under pressure; under duress; or living up to the expectations of someone else. When you do something you don't want to do, you will always feel upset, distressed, annoyed, irritated, unsettled, anxious, angry, physically or emotionally drained after it.

In a controlling / emotionally abusive relationship your partner might be forcing you to do things. Despite you not wanting to do it, you might find that you are talking yourself into certain situations and saying "yes" to things just to keep the peace or avoid confrontation.

Examples might be:
- Attending social events you don't want to attend.
- Going places you don't want to visit or be at.

- Going on a holiday that you don't want to go on.
- Eating in restaurants you don't like.
- Socialising with people you don't want to be around.
- Doing activities that you don't want to be involved in.
- Doing housework when you are feeling exhausted or tired.
- Spending money on items that you don't want to spend it on.
- Dressing in outfits or attire that you are not comfortable with.
- Behaving in a particular manner that is not normal or natural for you.
- Sexual acts you don't feel comfortable with.

Ask yourself:
- In this relationship, do I find myself saying yes to things I don't want to do?
- How do I feel when I say yes?
- How do I feel after the activity / experience?
- Why do I say yes?
- What would happen if I said no?
- How would my partner react if I said no to something?
- How would my life change if I started saying no?

If, by answering the above questions, you realise that you are saying yes to things because you are scared; fearful; worried; feeling intimidated; feel like you have no choice; feel that you will be rocking the boat; or think it is not worth the headache of saying no - then all these are signs that you are in a controlling / emotionally abusive relationship.

Fait**h**

Happiness

Happiness is not a privilege. It is your birth right and you are allowed to be happy.

I am not saying that you have to feel happy 100% of the time as this is an unrealistic expectation. Life events, life stresses or certain life experiences will take place which can make you feel off kilter and not your usual self. If however, your reason for unhappiness is your partner and your relationship, then this is something that may need to be addressed.

You can't expect to be happy all the time in a relationship. However, if you feel that you are spending more time within the relationship feeling unhappy rather than happy then this is a sign that your relationship needs attention.

It is not always easy to accept that you are unhappy within a relationship. I have seen individuals and come across many clients who are in complete denial and avoidance about their relationship not working. They are not ready to accept and acknowledge that something isn't right in the relationship.

Once you acknowledge that something isn't working or you say it out loud then it becomes real. When it becomes real there is no hiding from it. When there is no hiding from it then the issue requires attention or fixing, which can be a scary or daunting concept. In some cases there is also a practical implication of leaving the relationship e.g. house, property, finance, children, child care, disruption to family life.

There is no doubt that it is difficult to accept and acknowledge that a relationship isn't working but as time goes on, it will be much more difficult to continue staying within an unhappy relationship. You will begin to feel the impact of it both physically and emotionally.

So how do you know if your relationship is making you feel unhappy?

Close your eyes, take a deep breath and, make a promise to yourself that you will be as honest as you can with yourself. No one is listening and no one is judging you so answer the questions freely. You are not expected to do anything with the answers and nor is this a prompt for you to leave your relationship. No one can make you do that unless you are ready to do so. At this point in time all you are doing is gaining a better understanding of how you are feeling within your relationship.

Ask yourself:

- On a scale of 1 - 10 how happy does my relationship make me? (10 being the happiest)
- What areas of my relationship make me unhappy?
- What is it about my relationship that makes me unhappy?
- When did I notice this unhappiness?
- Where do I feel this unhappiness in my body?
- What have I done to address this unhappiness?
- What would help me address this unhappiness?
- What impact is this unhappiness having on other areas of my life?
- On a scale of 1 – 10, what are the chances of my unhappiness improving anytime soon? (10 being a strong chance)
- If the unhappiness doesn't improve, what are my options going forward?
- Who can I speak to about this unhappiness and who will understand?

The purpose of this exercise is to prompt you to reflect on your existing relationship and give consideration to what needs your attention. Just by answering these questions, you have taken a step out of the denial and avoidance stage. This is the first and most important step when it comes to creating any change in life. Well done!

Health

When we are feeling unhappy in life due to a relationship that is controlling / emotionally abusive, it is inevitable that our physical health will be affected.

Some of the physical symptoms to look out for are the following:
- Headaches.
- Constantly ill.
- Picking up colds / flus more so than normal.
- Weakened immune system.
- Stomach problems e.g. indigestion, irritable bowel syndrome, gastrointestinal problems.
- Skin problems e.g. rashes, breakouts, eczema.
- Changes in your skin complexion e.g. skin appearing dull or greyish complexion.
- Aches and pains in the body.
- Back problems.
- Pain in lower back.
- Tightness, stiffness or pain in shoulders, neck or upper back area.
- Grinding your teeth.

- Sore jaw upon waking up which could be due to grinding your teeth in sleep.
- Bruises gained as a result of walking into things because you are preoccupied with things running through your head and not paying attention to where you are going.
- Bruising gained as a result of weakened or poor immune system.
- Cuts or bruises taking longer to heal.
- Tiredness, fatigue or exhaustion.
- Heart palpitations.
- Increased heart rate.
- Fluttering in your chest.
- Tightness in your chest.
- Difficulty breathing.
- Dizziness, lightheaded or feeling a bit spaced out.
- Numbness, tingling or cold sensation in arms and legs.
- Pins and needles in arms and legs.
- Hot / cold flushes (common symptom of anxiety).
- High blood pressure.
- Feeling sick / nauseous.

Which of the symptoms do you notice from the previous list? Write them down.

Ask yourself:
- When did I first become aware of these symptoms?
- Have the symptoms got worse or better as time has gone on?
- What or who makes the symptoms worse?
- What or who makes the symptoms better?
- When was the last time I didn't have any of these symptoms to deal with?
- Have any of these symptoms been triggered off in the past as a result of relationships?
- What were those relationships like?
- How did I end or get out of those relationships?
- What would life be like if I didn't have these symptoms to constantly deal with it?

This section is about making you aware of the impact that your relationship is having on your physical health. We may choose to ignore what is going on inside our minds, however it is much harder to ignore physical changes that can occur within our body as a result of being in an unhealthy relationship.

Understanding how the relationship is impacting on your physical health can be a wakeup call as up until that point you maybe didn't even realise the gravitas of the situation.

The physical changes are your body's way of getting you to stop, to address the source of the stress, and create changes that will help you to feel better.

Hurt

In a controlling / emotionally abusive relationship, you will experience comments, behaviours or experiences that will leave you feeling hurt. This hurt can be delivered by the controller / abuser in many different ways such as:

- Criticising your appearance.
- Finding faults in your behaviour.
- Criticising you on your choices.
- Mocking you / making fun of you.
- Cracking jokes about you directly or indirectly in front of others.
- Judging you.
- Telling you that your opinions are not important, stupid or don't matter.
- Talking over you.
- Making decisions that affect you both but without checking with you first.
- Making decisions for you.
- Telling you what to do and how to do it.
- Embarrassing you in front of others.

- Humiliating you.
- Offending you / making offensive comments.
- Talking about you to others.
- Sharing private and personal stories about you to others.
- Telling others about your secrets or information that is personal to you.
- Comparing you to others and commenting on how you should be more like them.
- Questioning you and making you feel that there is something wrong with you.
- Making reference to things you have shared in the past.

I worked with a client who was experiencing relationship problems. In the past, my client had been in relationships that were physically abusive, something which she had shared with her current partner. During an argument her partner would make statements like:

"No wonder your ex beat you up."

"I can see why your ex hit you."

"You deserved that punch."

"Have you learnt nothing from your beatings."

I was both shocked and hurt on behalf of my client. However, I don't think she even realised how awful and wrong those comments actually were. I asked her what she thought of those statements and how they made her feel, to which she replied "Nothing, I am used to hearing those statements. Sometimes I think he might be right."

This scenario is all too familiar for me in my line of work. When in a controlling / emotionally abusive relationship, it is not uncommon for you to become immune to the hurtful comments. The more you hear these hurtful comments, the more normal and accepted they become within the relationship. You may consciously switch off your reaction to these comments however, subconsciously, you will still be affected. What happens is that the "hurt" manifests into a different emotion instead such as:

- Anger.
- Frustration.
- Irritation.
- Annoyance.
- Resentment.
- Bitterness.
- Hatred.
- Numbness.

- Hopelessness.
- Helplessness.
- Despair.
- Anguish.
- Self-loathing.
- Low self-esteem.
- Low self-confidence.
- Low self-worth.

These are just some of the signs that you **are** hurting, without even realising that you are.

Ask yourself:
- What feelings do I relate to?
- How long have I been feeling them?
- What is the cause of these feelings?
- What makes these feelings go away?
- If these feelings could talk, what would they be saying to me?

The purpose of this section is to make you aware of the hurt that you might, knowingly or unknowingly, be masking under other emotions. This section is also about alerting you to the different ways in which your partner could be hurting you mentally and emotionally.

None of this is acceptable so don't fool yourself by saying "Yeh but I have never been hit" or "it has never been physical" or "I feel physically safe".

Being hurt mentally or emotionally is not any better than being hurt physically. You don't have to put up with it and nor should you be feeling grateful that the hurt is mental / emotional and not physical. All forms of hurt inflicted within a relationship are wrong and should not be a part of any healthy relationship.

Heal

Healing is an important part of moving on in life from an upsetting or traumatic experience. Only once we have healed can we let go of any feelings that are attached to the upsetting or traumatic experience. If we had a physical injury, we would take the necessary precautions to ensure that we increased chances of a full recovery. This would entail cleaning the wound; covering / bandaging the wound to ensure it does not get infected; plaster / cast if required; and in certain injuries it would involve physiotherapy to ensure that the body part is fully functioning again.

Our mind is no different. It requires the same amount of care, attention, time and patience. In order to heal our mind, we need the support of the right people; the right circumstances; the right surroundings; and the right conditions around us.

Healing will help you to anchor / ground yourself, allowing you to think rationally, logically and calmly rather than emotionally, irrationally or chaotically. If you are thinking clearly and calmly it will enable you to make sense of your existing situation better, resulting in you being able to make the necessary decisions or take the next steps that are required.

Some of the things you can do to help you heal are:

Exercise

Any exercise that will increase your heart rate will burn off the adrenaline in your bloodstream. Excess adrenaline within your body will make you feel overwhelmed, emotional and burnt out. Burning off this adrenaline to eliminate it from your body will enable you to feel more settled within yourself. You don't need to be an athlete, as little as 20 minutes, 3 times a week is enough for you to start noticing and feeling a difference.

Pick an activity that you enjoy e.g. walking, jogging, swimming, running, dancing, fitness classes. There are plenty to choose from but whatever you pick, it has to be something that you enjoy and can fit into your existing schedule. If not, then you will find it difficult to stick to it.

Breathing Exercise

Overthinking and overanalysing can create burnout, exhaustion and leave you feeling drained. One of the miracle cures for reigning this in is to do a breathing exercise. It is a simple exercise of breathing in through your nose and breathing out through your mouth. You are not counting, meditating, or visualising anything.

Find a quiet place to yourself or a place that you will not be disturbed for 5 minutes. Inhale through your nose until you feel your lungs fill up with air. Once you feel that your lungs have fully filled up with air, I want you to exhale from your mouth, pushing all the air out, almost as though you are blowing out candles on a cake.

This breathing exercise should be carried out daily, every morning and every evening, because it will set you up for the day and also help you wind down at the end of the day. This breathing exercise is vital and should be carried out daily for 5 minutes every morning and night. You can increase this time later on down the line if you wish. For now, 5 minutes is enough, as even that will prove to feel like quite a long time.

Should or want?
Before you engage in an activity ask yourself whether you are doing it because you want to or because you feel you "should" be doing it. In life, most people will do things because they feel under pressure, feel guilty, feel bad, or feel obliged to do something. There is a fear of letting others down, disappointing people, or coming across as

not coping. It is these fears and insecurities that can cause you to do things that your heart is not in.

You will find yourself saying:
- "Just get on with it."
- "Keep going."
- "You have to just get on with it."
- "I can't stop."
- "I don't have a choice."
- "I'll get over it."
- "I'll be fine."
- "I'll be ok once I'm there."
- "Just put a brave face on."
- "Just smile through it."
- "It'll take my mind off things."
- "It'll be a distraction."
- "If I stop now, I'll never be able to get back up."
- "It feels like I am giving up."
- "I don't want this to get the better of me."

These may seem like words of encouragement and strength but don't be deceived. These statements are actually ways of avoiding dealing with what you are going through or experiencing.

When we are healing from a traumatic / upsetting experience, our mind needs time to process what has happened, to analyse it, to understand it, and to make sense of it all in our own unique way.

In order to do this, you will need time out, you will need to rest, you may need to be anti-social for a while, you might have to slow things down or remove some things from your daily routine. At this stage, it would be helpful to get involved only in activities that you actually want to get involved in rather than feeling under pressure to carry on in life as nothing has happened.

Now you might be thinking about the practicality of this rule of life and how it is not a realistic plan for the long term. You might have kids that require looking after, you might have a demanding job, you might be going through a busy period in life, you may have others dependent on you. I understand all that and I am not asking you to incorporate this rule and make it a permanent part of your life.

This strategy is for the short term and it is there to aid your healing through a critical stage of your recovery. If you keep putting pressure on yourself to carry on in life as though nothing has happened, then you are hindering your healing process. It is the equivalent of running on a broken leg and then wondering why it doesn't heal. Until you begin to feel emotionally stronger, adopting the rule of "Am I doing this because I want to or because I feel I should be?" will be in your best interest.

Other tips that will help you to heal:
- Ask yourself, what do I need right now? e.g. sleep, rest, be left alone, some time out, a break, breathing space, to feel relaxed, a massage etc
- How can I make that happen?
- Who can help me make that happen?
- What would stop that from happening?
- How can I overcome this obstacle?
- Remind yourself that this is a temporary stage and you won't feel like this forever.
- Tell yourself that self-care is not selfish.

This section is all about helping you heal as much as you can whilst you are within this controlling / emotionally abusive relationship.

This healing will help anchor / ground you enough to think clearly, calmly and give you the respite that you need in order to help you decide on your next steps. This section should not be used to develop coping strategies to continue staying within the controlling / emotionally abusive relationship.

Hate

In a controlling / emotionally abusive relationships I notice that the person who is experiencing the control / emotional abuse can sometimes develop feelings of hate towards themselves. This is not only sad to see but also an emotion which is completely displaced.

The controller / abuser has made you feel so unlovable; unwanted; undesirable; unworthy; invaluable; and flawed that self-hate becomes a feeling that is inevitable. The hate is present because you will be annoyed at yourself – some of the commonly made statements are:

- "I'm so angry at myself for getting into this situation."
- "I should have known better."
- "What's wrong with me?"
- "How did I not see this?"
- "Maybe it's my fault?"
- "I feel so stupid."
- "I feel like such an idiot."
- "I feel so weak."
- "I used to be so strong."
- "I don't even know who I am."

- "I feel so pathetic."
- "I feel so embarrassed."
- "I'm ashamed of myself."
- "I can't even look at myself in the mirror."

I wrote this section because it is very important for you to know that this situation is NOT YOUR FAULT. There is nothing that you have said or done to warrant being treated in a way that is making you emotionally and physically unwell.

You will have been drip fed over the course of that relationship that you are imperfect; you are flawed; you are to blame; you are at fault, but this is part of the emotional manipulation and control. It is NOT TRUE!

Ask yourself:
- Who else in my life treats me this way?
- If I was so undesirable, unlovable, unwanted etc then why did my partner decide to be in a relationship with me in the first place?
- How would my family / friends that love and care for me feel if they found out that I hated myself?

- What would they say to me?
- When I have the hateful thoughts running through my mind, whose voice is running in my head?
- Does the voice belong to me or my partner?
- What do I gain from hating myself?
- What would make me stop hating myself?

Hate is a strong emotion and will blind you from seeing anything clearly. It will distort and obscure your reality. These questions listed above are not a magic wand but they will help you to work through the feelings of hate; untangle them; and explore the reasons for them.

Moving away from self-hate will help you to see things for the way that they are and perhaps help you to accept that you are not to blame for any of this.

Help

Relationships require hard work, dedication, commitment, compromise and effort from both sides. What happens when this contribution is just from one side? Is that fair? Is it right? Is it acceptable?

In a controlling / emotionally abusive relationship, what often becomes evident is that there is one person who is giving and putting in more than the other one. There will be one person running around doing everything whilst the other person doesn't have to change or alter their schedule whatsoever. No help, assistance or support is offered. If the person doing all the running around asks for help, they are shut down by being told:

- "You are always nagging."
- "You are constantly having a go."
- "Always on about something."
- "Why are you always on my case?"
- "You are so annoying."
- "Why can't you do it yourself."
- "I'm busy."

- "I can't be bothered"
- "I'm too tired."
- "I have to do everything here."
- "Why are you being so lazy."

Over the years, I have heard of various ways in which this one-sided relationship takes place. Here are some examples:

- You are constantly cleaning, cooking or doing other housework.
- You are the one that is constantly doing the house chores even if you are unwell.
- You are rushing around doing things whilst your partner just sits there doing nothing or is otherwise engaged with tv, phone, devices.
- You are the one paying for everything or covering a majority of the financial expenditure.
- If children are involved, you might be the one that is constantly rushing around after them without any help or support from your partner.
- The other common thing is that you are the one who is left to deal with the disciplining of the children whilst all the

fun activities involve your partner.
- You are the one that is constantly having to compromise.
- You are the one that is constantly having to change their plans to accommodate your partner, even if it means at the expense of your emotional health and wellbeing.
- What you want to do or where you want to go is never taken into consideration.
- Your partner might avoid doing certain tasks or taking certain responsibilities by saying that they don't know how to do it or in some cases even blame you for not liking the way they do things so there is no point in them doing anything.

Ask yourself:

- Do I feel that my partner and I contribute equally within the relationship?
- Who does the most in the relationship?
- What are the reasons for this?
- How do I feel about this dynamic?
- How would I like things to be?
- What would happen if I discussed this with my partner?
- What can I do to change the dynamic of the relationship so that I feel it is fair?

A healthy relationship is about two individuals putting in equal amounts of hard work; effort; dedication; and commitment. I understand that this is not always possible as there will be times that due to circumstance or life events, one person will have to contribute more than the other. However, when both partners are happy, healthy, able and capable, then the effort should be from both sides.

Hope

A controlling / emotionally abusive relationship will make you feel stuck, trapped and suffocated. The longer you stay in this relationship the worse you will feel. As time goes on, you will hit a dip and the downward spiral begins where you will be encompassed by a range of feelings such as depression, despair, dread, fatigue, defeat, doom, hopelessness or helplessness.

Subconsciously you will know what is happening and how you are feeling within the relationship, isn't right. That sinking or niggly feeling in the pit of your stomach will tell you that. However, you won't know what you have to do or how you can make it stop.

At times like this what one needs is light at the end of the tunnel - hope that this feeling can come to an end; hope that you can feel different; hope that you might be able to feel free once again; hope that you might be able to escape a relationship that is toxic and unhealthy for your wellbeing.

In order to generate feelings of hope, you will have to mentally move yourself into the future and picture what your reality will be like. The purpose behind this exercise is to give you incentive, motivation and the drive to make changes in your existing situation.

Make a plan:

- Where will I go once I leave my current situation?
- Who will I go see?
- Where will I stay?
- What will I do for money?
- How will I make it happen?
- Who will / can help me?
- What will I do in the new situation?
- What reaction do I expect from my partner?
- How will I deal with this reaction?
- What can I do to ensure that I am safe, secure and not in any danger?

Planning and preparing is key. It will give you the focus, confidence and direction that you need. More importantly, it will give you hope during a time when you might be feeling at rock bottom and thinking that there is no way out.

Closing remarks

It is tempting to talk to others about your situation and seek advice about what you should do. However the advice given to you by this person(s) will be influenced by their own life experiences; fears; insecurities; or anxieties.

No one can comment on your relationship or tell you what to do unless they have been in that relationship too. The only person that can make a decision about what to do and what the next steps are is YOU.

This is why I have written and structured this book in the way that it is. This book encourages you to reflect on your relationship; focus on your feelings; and increase your awareness about the impact that it is having on you. The answers to the listed questions will empower you with the knowledge, clarity and understanding that you need to make the right decision for you, at the right time.

In times of doubt, fear, confusion or hesitation, I want you to remember that your feelings are your compass in life. If something doesn't feel right, it probably ISN'T right. If something feels wrong, it probably IS wrong. If you feel unhappy, you probably HAVE a reason for it. If you have an unsettled feeling in your gut, you AREN'T imagining it.

Have faith in your feelings and use the "faith" in this book to help you build your self-confidence; self-esteem; and self-worth.

This book is not the magic answer to your situation however it *can* be the catalyst for change in your situation. That change should be one that enables you to live a life that is happier, healthier and stress-free because you deserve it just as much as anyone else.

About the author

Kamalyn is a professionally trained, qualified and experienced Cognitive Behaviour Therapist. She is a fully registered and accredited member of the BACP (British Association for Counselling and Psychotherapy).

Since 2012, Kamalyn has worked with a diverse range of individuals from all walks of life helping them to deal with emotional distress caused by abuse, anxiety, depression, eating disorders, grief, low self-confidence, low self-esteem, marital difficulties, stress and post-traumatic stress disorder. She has also worked with various organisations from the public, private and voluntary sectors by assisting their employees with work related stress, improving work performance, absence management and confidence building.

Kamalyn believes that knowledge is power. She therefore works closely with the client to help them gain an understanding of how to manage their thoughts, feelings and behaviours. Clients are further empowered by introducing them to tools, techniques and strategies that will enable them to take control of the situation that is distressing them.

The aim is for the client to make the necessary changes within their life to feel happier, healthier and stress free.

To find out more about Kamalyn; the work she does; or her services as a therapist, visit her website on:

www.keytherapies.org.uk

Printed in Poland
by Amazon Fulfillment
Poland Sp. z o.o., Wrocław